Kittens Don't Eat Jam!

By Sally Cowan

Janet and Dad got lots of plums at the market.

They made plum jam in a big pot.

"We can put the jam
on crumpets!" said Janet.

"Or on bagels!" said Dad.

Velvet the kitten was outside hunting crickets in the garden.

He came back in through an open window.

Janet and Dad did not see the sneaky little kitten.

Dad put the jam in some jars and left them to cool.

Janet went out to the garden.

"Time to eat, Velvet!" she yelled.

Janet did not know that Velvet was inside.

He had just woken up, and now he wanted some food!

The hungry little kitten jumped up to the jam jars!

"Velvet, no!" yelled Dad.

But Velvet had taken a big slurp of jam!

He spat it out.

Jam is too sweet for kittens!

"Get **down**, Velvet!" yelled Dad.

Velvet shot off like a rocket!

In his rush, he kicked a jar!

CRASH!

Janet saw the smashed jar.

Sticky blobs of jam were
on the carpet!

"Oh, Velvet!" she said.

"Velvet, you little piglet!"
said Janet.

Janet got a packet
of Velvet's food.

"**This** is your food, Velvet,"
said Janet.
"Kittens don't eat jam!"

CHECKING FOR MEANING

1. What did Dad and Janet make in the big pot? *(Literal)*

2. How did Velvet sneak into the house? *(Literal)*

3. How did Velvet know there was food on the bench? *(Inferential)*

EXTENDING VOCABULARY

crumpets and bagels	What do these words mean? What do we usually spread on these food items?
Velvet	Why do you think Janet called her kitten *Velvet*? What is velvet? How does it feel? How would the kitten feel to touch?
sticky	Look at the word *sticky*. Discuss that the *y* makes a long /ee/ sound. Can you think of other words that end in *y* with the long /ee/ sound? E.g. tricky, picky.

MOVING BEYOND THE TEXT

1. Have you ever made jam? Who helped you? Which fruit did you use?

2. Why do kittens like chasing crickets and other insects? Do they catch them? Why?

3. Why do you think Janet said, "Velvet, you little piglet!"?

4. Where do kittens like to sleep? Why?

THE SCHWA

| a | e | i | o | u |

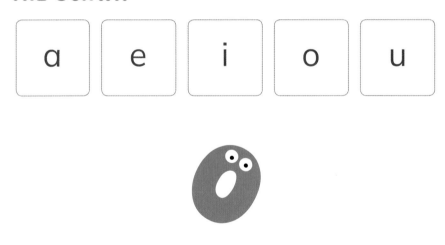

PRACTICE WORDS

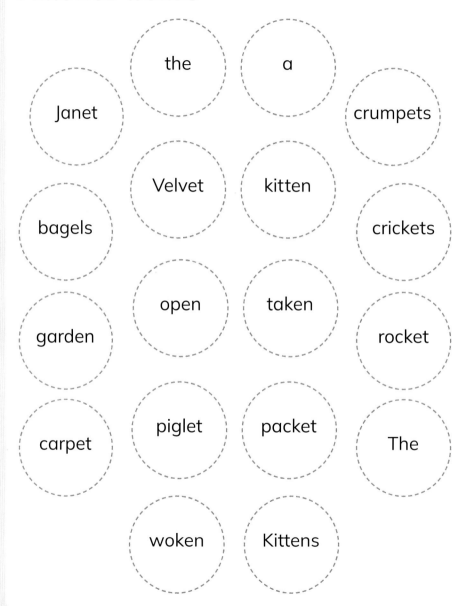

the

a

Janet

crumpets

Velvet

kitten

bagels

crickets

open

taken

garden

rocket

piglet

packet

carpet

The

woken

Kittens